A BEGINNER'S GUIDE TO GROWTH STOCK INVESTING

JAMES PATTERSENN JR.

www.theintelligentinvestorhub.com

CONTENTS

DISCLAIMER

This book was published for educational purposes, and it's not intended to provide specific personalized advice. It's sold with the understanding that the author or publisher is not engaged in rendering legal, accounting, investment or other professional services. Investing in stocks and the stock market involves varying degrees of risk, and there's no assurance that a specific stock, investment principle or investment strategy will be profitable for an individual, group or organization. All information contained in this book was gathered from sources believed to be reliable, but neither the author nor the publisher can accept responsibility for its accuracy.

The author or publisher specifically denies any responsibility for liability, loss, or risk, professional or otherwise, which is incurred as a consequence, directly or indirectly, of the use and application of any of the contents of this book.

ISBN 978-1-7365803-5-6 (Softcover)
ISBN 978-1-7365803-4-9 (eBook)

OTHER BOOKS BY JAMES PATTERSENN JR

You Can Invest Like A Stock Market Pro: How to Use Simple and Powerful Strategies of the World's Greatest Investors to Build Wealth

Would you like to forget about your money problems and finally live a life of wealth and prosperity? Learn how to apply approaches used by the best stock investors in the world to consistently build wealth over decades of investing.

Now That You Can Invest Like a Pro: More Principles and Strategies for Building Wealth Like the World's Greatest Investors

Are you ready to learn time-tested investing strategies that actually work? Author James Pattersenn again draws on thousands of hours of stock investing research and decades of stock investing experience to teach you investment strategies to help you make money with stocks.

Common Sense Investing With Stock Screeners: Make Stock Investing a Safe Bet With the Right Tools

Would you like to have the perfect all-in-one stock screening guide that you could constantly use to find the most profitable stocks in the market? Simply follow the step-by-step instructions and expert strategies found in this stock screeners guide for beginners. Your fortune is waiting for you – what are you waiting for?

100 Stocks That a Young Warren Buffett Might Buy: Proven Methods for Buying Stocks and Building Wealth Like Warren Buffett and Charlie Munger

Want to learn the most important stock buying guidelines that Warren Buffett and Charlie Munger use to pick stocks that will outperform the stock market by large margins and build wealth incrementally over time? Join the author as he applies Buffett's and Munger's more than 60 years of incredible stock market expertise in a fascinating (and potentially extremely profitable) experiment.

Common Sense Investing With Index Funds: How to Build Wealth, Achieve Financial Freedom, and Outperform Most Amateur and Professional Investors Without Really Trying!

Are you tired of your 9 to 5 job that earns you just enough money to pay the bills? Are you interested in investing, but you are afraid that you will lose all your money? With this guide, you will discover the simple path to wealth and financial freedom with index fund investing.

YOUR FREE GIFT

Thanks for buying my book. As a way of showing my appreciation, I'd like to give you something. It won't cost you a penny! It's my PDF report titled *5 Stocks That Warren Buffett Would Love.*

I'd like you to have a copy with my compliments.
Contained within this report are:

- 5 wonderful companies that Warren Buffett might buy today if given the opportunity.
- The specific criteria for picking Buffett-type stocks via value investing.
- Great companies that are practically guaranteed to grow and deliver big returns well beyond the pandemic!

Claim your copy of *5 Stocks That Warren Buffett Would Love* by clicking the link below and joining my mailing list. As added bonus to being on my mailing list, I will alert you when I release a new book. Since my new releases are usually free or selling at a steep discount for the first 24 to 48 hours, you'll be the first to know.

https:/ mailchi.mp/b65776af6219/5-stocks-warren-buffett-would-love

1

THE SKY IS THE LIMIT

Growth stock investing can be highly rewarding for the investor that has the time and the temperament to let this amazing strategy work. Philip A. Fisher, a pioneer in growth stock investing and considered one of the greatest investors of all time, had this to say about growth stock investing. "The young growth stock offers by far the greatest possibility of gain. Sometimes this can amount up to several thousand percent in a decade."

On January 2, 2020, Novavax, Inc., started the year with a trading price of $3.99 per share. During the year, Novavax shares rose to a high of more than $181 per share. At the close of 2020, the shares had fallen to $111.51, yet even at that price the stock returned 2695% for the year. To put that return performance into perspective, every $1000 invested in Novavax at the beginning of 2020 was worth $27,950 at the end of the year. Of course Novavax wasn't alone when it came to some amazing returns in 2020. For example, here are some other stocks that had some impressive gains in 2020: Vaxart (up 1606%), Beam Global (up 1358%), NIO (up 1,103%), Cardiff Oncology (up 1,311%), and Blink Charging (up 2,332%).

The point that I'm making is that it only takes owning one or a few of the right growth stocks for you to be financially set for life; never needing to worry about money again. When it comes to growth stocks, remember that earnings growth drives stock prices and are the driving force of growth stocks.

I'm not recommending that you buy Novavax or any of the stocks that have been mentioned, but I simply want you to see what can happen with growth stocks. Great investor, Peter Lynch said, "If you invest $1000 in a stock, all you can lose is $1000, but you stand to gain $10,000 or even $50,000 over time if you're patient." He went on to say, "It only takes a handful of big winners to make a lifetime of investing worthwhile."

Once you have read this beginner's guide to growth stock investing, it's my hope that you will be better equipped to identify and purchase those big winners that will help you achieve financial freedom for life. After all, when it comes to the returns of growth stocks, the sky is the limit!

2

BUILDING WEALTH WITH GROWTH STOCKS

G rowth stocks are stocks of fast-growing businesses that are expected to generate above-average revenue and earnings. The increases in revenue and earnings are very important because they translate into greater returns for the shareholders. These fast-growing businesses tend to be small to mid-sized companies. They have significant room for growth in size, revenue, and most importantly, earnings.

Let's look at a comparison between The Coca-Cola Company (KO) and National Beverage Corporation (FIZZ). As of today, January 28, 2021, The Coca-Cola Company has a market capitalization of $210. 5 billion, meaning that if you were to purchase all of The Coca-Cola Company's outstanding shares; it would cost you that amount to buy the company. At a market capitalization of $210.5 billion, we can see that The Coca-Cola Company is very large. National Beverage Corporation's current market capitalization is $8.2 billion. By comparison, The Coca-Cola Company is twenty-six times larger than National Beverage Corporation.

Both companies are well-managed and both have generated positive earnings. Because National Beverage Corporation is a much smaller company, it stands the best chance of achieving the greatest increases in growth when compared to The Coca-Cola Company, but a company's size alone is never the best indicator of its growth potential. It's necessary to look at some historical performance data along with analysts' estimates before we can make the best choice or estimate. Looking a little more closely at other financial data, we can see that The Coca-Cola Company managed to grow its earnings at an annual rate of 5.30% for the past five years and analysts estimate that the company will grow its earnings at an annual rate of 2.18% over the next five years. National Beverage Corporation achieved an annual earnings growth rate of 21.40% during the last five years and analysts estimate that earnings will grow at an annual rate of 25.56% over the next five years.

As you can see, National Beverage Corporation has the best opportunity for the greatest increase in growth when compared to The Coca-Cola Company. It's much easier to grow an $8 billion company into an $80 billion company than it is to grow a $200 billion company into a $2 trillion company.

In 1999, Warren Buffett told the shareholders at the annual meeting for Berkshire Hathaway that he could generate 50% annual returns for the shareholders, if only he had less money to invest. Having smaller amounts of money to invest gives you and me an advantage, even over Buffett and Munger, since we are able to invest in the smaller, faster-growing companies that have the potential to provide the greatest returns to investors. Buffett and Munger have to move large amounts of money that investing in the small, fast-growing companies, to which I am referring, would hardly make any kind of impact on Berkshire Hathaway's portfolio. In other words, if Buffett or Munger invested in smaller businesses, this investment would have very little effect on the total return of the portfolio. It probably would not be worth their time.

Although I'm mainly referring to small and mid-sized companies, there are companies with large market capitalizations that also qualify as growth stocks. So, don't hesitate to invest in those as well—as long as the price is right.

3

LOOKING FOR THE BIG WINNERS OF TOMORROW

To discover the big winners of tomorrow in growth stocks, we need to identify emerging growth opportunities or revolutionary trends taking place around the world. By doing so, we are more capable of identifying those companies that are best positioned to take advantage of those opportunities or trends.

By searching for companies that will achieve high earnings growth that's sustainable, we are on our way to finding tomorrow's big winners. Research has shown that earnings growth drives a stock's price and is almost 100% correlated with a stock's performance over the long-term. In addition, the big winners usually start out as small companies with market capitalizations of less than $1 billion that grow into large companies.

Some long-term trends taking place now that will be very profitable for investors are listed next: Robotics, artificial intelligence (AI), computer viruses, chronic disease, global pandemics, crime, identity theft, internet gambling, healthcare, smoking cessation, internet of things, autonomous vehicles, work from home, renewable energy, etc. I could go on and on, but I don't think that I need to.

There are so many profitable areas in which we could look for growth stocks now. Tomorrow's big winners are out there, but we've got to be willing to put in the time and energy needed to find them. The best part is that the internet has made the entire research process a whole lot easier and faster. With today's technology, we have absolutely no excuse when it comes to being capable of searching for the big winners of tomorrow in growth stocks. One thing is for certain, if we don't search for tomorrow's big winners, we are highly unlikely to ever find them.

4

12 PRINCIPLES FOR INVESTING LIKE A PRO

There are some simple, yet powerful principles that can help you succeed in stock market investing. When studying and researching some of the world's most successful investors, I discovered that these twelve principles tended to be universal among them, which means that these time-tested principles are very important for long-term investment success. Although the principles may appear to be simple or common sense, the majority of those that invest in the stock market fail to use them. I believe those investors that are willing to adhere to these principles will be very happy with the long-term performance of their portfolios.

Principle #1: Stick with the stocks of businesses that you understand.

If you don't understand a business, don't purchase its stock. Investors are more likely to pick better-performing stocks if they purchase the stocks of businesses that they understand. Usually those easy-to-understand, boring businesses are the ones that make money year after year. It has been said many times that a good investment is usually a boring one.

Principle #2: Be a long-term investor.

Warren Buffett has said that if you don't plan on holding a stock for 10 years, you have no business holding it for 10 minutes. Holding a stock for the long-term is the most effective way to maximize your return since a stock's earnings will usually increase dramatically over time along with its book value. These increases will result in the stock trading at a significantly higher price over the long-term and if the stock pays dividends, the dividends are likely to grow consistently also.

Principle #3 Try to purchase stocks when they are trading at low P/E ratios.

Look for stocks trading significantly below their average annual price-to-earnings ratio for the last 7 to 10 years. The price-to-earnings ratio is normally referred to simply as the P/E ratio.

The equation that follows demonstrates how the P/E of a stock is determined:

$$\frac{\text{Price-Per-Share}}{\text{Earnings-Per-Share}} = \text{P/E Ratio}$$

For example, a stock is currently trading on the market for $40 per share. It has $2 in total estimated earnings for the year. The calculation would look like this:

$$\frac{\$40}{\$2} = 20 \text{ or a P/E of } 20$$

The P/E for the stock is 20. If this P/E is lower than the average annual P/E of the stock for the last 7 to 10 years, then the stock is probably cheap based on what investors have been willing to pay for the shares in the past. Another important thing that you should know is not to avoid stocks just because they are trading at what appears to be high P/E ratios. History has shown us that many high P/E ratio stocks that seemed to be too expensive have proven to be long-term winners. A good example of this kind of stock is Amazon.com, Inc.

Principle #4: Buy low and sell high.

Most investors tend to buy high and sell low, doing the exact opposite of what they should do. They buy an overvalued stock and when there's a market sell-off, they panic and sell too. This results in them selling the stock for much less than they paid for it. For intelligent investors, this market sell-off is a great time to buy excellent stocks at a discount.

Principle #5: Don't buy a stock just because it's cheap.

Everyone would love to be able to purchase a stock for $1 and watch it skyrocket to $40 before selling it, but that rarely happens. If a stock is very cheap or has recently lost most of its value, then something fundamental to the success of the business has other investors concerned. Look for undervalued, high-quality stocks instead of cheap stocks, and never buy a stock because it used to be $40 a share and now trades for $2 per share. If a stock's price has been on a continuous downhill slope and the stock has lost most of its value, think long and hard before purchasing it.

Principle #6: Select stocks that have strong brand appeal.

Look for businesses that have strong brand appeal when purchasing stocks. A strong brand appeal gives them a durable competitive advantage over their competition. Examples are Nike, PepsiCo, Wal-Mart, Under Armour, and Walgreens. Almost everyone has heard of these businesses or has purchased the products that they sell. When consumers see a brand name, they expect to receive high-quality products at a fair price.

Principle #7: Diversify your portfolio.

Diversification is one of the most important elements necessary for successful investing. When it comes to stocks, you should never put all of your eggs in one basket. Diversification reduces risk and improves an investor's opportunity for a better return. For the growth stock investor, a diversified portfolio is one that consists of stocks from a variety of industries and sectors. For example, if you have decided to create a portfolio that will contain a total of five stocks, it would be unwise to hold five stocks from the same industry in that portfolio, such as five oil company stocks. The best and safest approach would be to purchase five stocks from five completely different industries. In doing so, if one or two of the industries suffer because of some economic turmoil, the other stocks s may not be affected much.

Principle #8: Keep your emotions in check.

Never make an investment decision that is based just on your feelings or emotions. Always get the facts before buying or selling a stock. Emotions are the cause of a lot of the stock market's volatility, but when the underlying factors are checked, most of the time nothing notable has changed in the stock market that warrants the volatility.

Principle #9: Watch out for greed.

Never allow greed to cause you to make very risky or foolish decisions when investing. It is the number one killer of an investor's wealth. It causes investors to make rash decisions without much thought or research. The smart investor is able to benefit from the greed of others.

Principle #10: Do your own homework.

This is a biggie when it comes to investing. Please do your own research before investing your hard-earned money into any investment. All too often, investors are willing to put their money into recommendations from individuals that have less knowledge about investing than themselves. I believe that you can do a much better job managing your portfolio and finances than many of the investment experts out there. Research has revealed that 90% of fund managers fail to outperform the market over the long-term. Unlike the investment adviser or fund manager that may have hundreds of accounts under management, you will only need to be concerned with your account and can therefore fully commit yourself to make the best choices and decisions concerning it.

Principle #11: Don't lose money.

This is exactly what's going to happen if you attempt to get-rich-quick or time the stock market. When investing in stocks, you must be able to cope with your investments falling drastically in price without you panicking and selling your stocks at a loss. It's not uncommon for very good stocks to fall 50% or more in value in any given year, and that's definitely not something I enjoy seeing. If it happens to you, your response should be to hang in there if you know that you have made the right choice. Better yet, buy some more of the stock if its fundamentals have not changed or have improved. Most importantly, have the goal and the determination to not lose any of your money from investing.

Principle #12: Be a patient investor.

The world's most successful investors did not amass their fortunes overnight. It took some time to do so. Time and the power of compounding are an investor's greatest allies. Warren Buffett has said, "The stock market is a device for transferring money from the impatient to the patient." So, as you strive to build wealth and achieve financial freedom, be sure to practice patience.

5

MARGIN OF SAFETY

Regardless of the type of investment strategy used by an investor whether its growth, value, contrarian, dividend, etc., I have discovered that *margin of safety* is one of the most important ingredients for investing successfully. Margin of safety is very easy to implement within almost any investment plan, program, or strategy.

A margin of safety is the difference between a stock's market price and its fair value. Again and again, as I studied the investment systems and strategies of some of the world's most successful investors, they especially had in common the following: Every one of them stressed the importance of purchasing a stock only when it was trading at a discount to its fair or intrinsic value. In other words, every one of them would only buy stocks that contained a margin of safety.

Since the fair value of a business is difficult to estimate with 100% accuracy, it's a good practice to attempt to purchase a stock when it's trading at a discount to its estimated fair value. The lower the purchase price of a stock, relative to its estimated fair value, the safer the investment becomes. In my use of margin of safety, I like to invest in companies whose stocks are trading at a minimum discount of 25% off their estimated fair value. The bigger the discount, the more I like the stock. For example, if I estimate that a specific stock has a fair value of $12, I will only purchase that stock when it can be bought for $9 or less per share in the market.

Throughout my research, I have found margin of safety recommendations of anywhere from 10 to 50%. As I have already mentioned, I prefer to buy a stock when it can be purchased at a discount of 25% or more off its estimated fair value. When it comes to investing, margin of safety is one, if not the most important element to take into consideration. This is true whether you are investing in stocks, bonds, real estate, commodities, a farm, or a laundromat. With each of these investments, margin of safety should be considered before one penny is spent. It's got to be there if you want to build great wealth through stock market investing. When it comes to growth stocks, the margin of safety is our primary method for reducing risk. So, it is of utmost importance to buy growth stocks with a margin of safety in their trading price.

6

INVESTMENT RISK

W hat is investment risk? The definition of investment risk that I like is found at Investopedia: *"The chance that an investment's actual return will be different than expected. Risk includes the possibility of losing some or all of the original investment."*

There are different types of risk when investing in stocks. In an article titled "The 3 Types of Investment Risk," Joshua Kennon addresses business risk, valuation risk, and force of sale risk. To keep things simple, the main risk that I'm concerned with is the loss of our money through investing. With any investment program, regardless of the type, there are no guarantees and you can lose money. I'll be the first to admit that investing in stocks is risky and the risk that I'm talking about is losing money.

Growth stock investing entails purchasing the stocks of faster-growing small and mid-sized companies at attractive prices, however, research indicates portfolios comprising only these fast growers may be more volatile and risky than most other types of portfolios such as large-cap blue-chip stock portfolios, or portfolios that contain a combination of stocks and bonds.

There are some things that investors can do to reduce risk to their portfolios, and many books have been written on that subject. I have learned that Index Funds can serve a very important purpose of reducing investment risk within the portfolios of some investors. Warren Buffett has said that some investors are better off putting their money into low-cost index funds such as the Vanguard S&P 500 Index Fund. He stated, "By periodically investing in an index fund, the know-nothing investors can actually outperform most investment professionals." Buffett's statement provides enough evidence that investing a portion of your wealth into an index fund is one way to reduce investment risk because of its low cost and the instant diversification it provides. The Motley Fool® staff believes that the index fund should be the foundation of a beginning or new investor's portfolio. In an article, the Motley Fool staff stated, "Little wonder that we think index funds should be the foundation of your portfolio. But for now, we simply recommend that for every dollar you put into stocks, you roll the same amount into an index fund." There are other actions that investors can take to reduce investment risk within their portfolio, such as:

- Determine how much investment risk you can handle and operate within that perimeter.
- Only invest money that you can truly afford to lose.
- Don't invest any money that you will need within five years into stocks.
- Create a portfolio that is diversified and contains 10-20 stocks.

- Only buy a stock when a margin of safety exists in its price.
- Do not participate in the frequent trading of stocks but invest for the long-term.
- Don't buy stocks on margin or through the use of a margin account.
- Create and use practice accounts before investing real money into stocks.
- Seek the advice of an investment professional with a proven track record of success.

Many investors confuse volatility and risk. Volatility is the fluctuations in a stock's price and other factors besides risk can result in a stock being highly volatile. Some stocks may display a lot of volatility, yet may not be as risky, as many of those stocks that have a history of low volatility. It's not uncommon for individual stocks to fluctuate 50% or more in price in any given year and this includes the stocks of some of the best companies in the United States. So, be careful not to classify a stock as high risk or low risk based solely on its volatility or lack thereof.

7

THE STOCK SCREENER

When it comes to trading or investing, things can get a little complex and/or aggravating, especially when it comes to picking the right stocks for your portfolio. Consider the fact that there are three major stock exchanges in the United States with no less than 2400 stocks listed on the New York Stock Exchange alone, and each of those companies that the stocks represent are different in their makeup. For example, their business prospects, their employees, their facilities, and their finances will be very different, and this only complicates the matter for investors or traders. Don't forget, we have not even included the companies that trade on the other two major exchanges here in the United States. If that's not enough to making picking stocks more complex, I don't know what is.

As an investor, I do acknowledge that the stock screener is my best friend when it comes to identifying potential investment candidates, by making the process less convoluted. If you are not already using screeners, once you start, you may just find yourself agreeing with me that the screener is indeed the investor's or trader's best friend. You may be asking "what in the heck is a stock screener?" The stock screener is a very important tool in my arsenal for wealth creation. A stock screener is a very powerful investment tool that scans a database to search for stocks that meet certain criteria, which have been specified by an investor or trader.

The main components of any screener are a database of companies (stocks), a set of variables, and a screening engine that functions much like a search engine on the internet. Screeners may vary from being very simple and basic, to much more complex. However, good screeners will allow you to search for companies using just about any criterion that's desired. Stock screeners may be standalone software programs or web-based programs. I use only the free, web-based screeners, and I think that a few of them are excellent, and several of the web-based screeners are free to use.

I have spent thousands of hours researching and studying stocks. The truth is that much of that time could have been put to better use, if only I had known about stock screeners when I started my research many years ago. With stock screeners, traders and investors are capable of analyzing hundreds of stocks in a very short time. This same process of analyzing stocks usually would have taken days or even weeks to perform before stock screeners were available, and that's no exaggeration!

I now greatly depend on stock screeners when I perform my research, and wouldn't want to be without them. Without the use of stock screeners, searching for stocks that meet the stringent criteria that I require, can be compared to searching for a needle in a haystack. Remember, just on the exchanges in the United States, there are thousands of stocks. Stock screeners save time by eliminating those companies that do not meet an investor's or trader's requirements.

A stock screener will generate a list of stocks that will need to be further studied, and is merely the first step. But, it is a very important step since it filters out stocks that don't meet your required criteria, and creates a list of stocks that do. Because each screener is different, the search parameters will vary somewhat.

Once you have run the stock screen, you will probably generate a large number of stocks that require additional research based on your investment program and/or strategies; quickly weeding out those stocks that do not belong on your list. Screening should never be used as a substitute for performing your research, and the stocks retrieved by a screener or screening tool should not be considered a buy list, but a thorough financial analysis should be performed on every stock before determining whether or not to purchase them.

8

SCREENING FOR WINNING GROWTH STOCKS

In this section, we will look at the screening criteria for picking winning growth stocks. To succeed as a growth stock investor, you've got to have a plan. There is an old saying, "If you fail to plan, you are planning to fail" and when investing in growth stocks that saying is also true. One of the most important aspects of any investment plan is the investment criteria used to select stocks that possess specific traits. Once you have completed the reading of this book, I believe that you will have discovered an effective plan for investing in winning growth stocks.

Even with the right plan in place, you've got to stay in the game to win it. Legendary investor, Peter Lynch said, "The key to making money in stocks is not getting scared out of them." So, even with growth stocks, the best way to make money with them is to hold them for the long-term and stick to your plan.

The criteria that will be explained is the same that I have relied on for several years in my research, and believe that it will be very useful for the beginner as well as the more advanced growth stock investor.

With time and experience, you may decide to change or modify the screening criteria explained here. Nevertheless, the criteria provided will certainly get you off to a good start when it comes to identifying winning growth stocks more easily while avoiding those stocks that appear to be candidates but really are not.

Now, we will look at the screening criteria that I use in my search for those growth stocks that possess tremendous growth potential and offer the greatest potential returns to investors:

- **The Company should be based in the U.S.** When it comes to growth stocks, I prefer to stay with companies based in the U.S. since they are more regulated and watched. Many foreign countries have much less stringent regulations when it comes to their stock markets which results in greater risk to those willing to invest in them.

- **The company should possess a minimum market capitalization of $300 million.** A $300 million company might seem large but it's really a very small company when we consider the fact that there are many companies with market caps of several hundred billion or more. With growth stocks, you want to find stocks that are small enough that they have much room to grow, yet they are not so small that they become very risky as investments.

- **The companies should have at least a ten-year history of consistent operations.** Even with growth stocks, you want to be investing in companies with a long-term history of consistent operations. By doing so, it will help you to avoid risky new companies that might not be around in a few years.

- **The company should be a non-commodity type that has a strong brand and/or franchise.** Commodity-type companies are very volatile and unpredictable. They are also cyclical in nature, meaning that their performance is directly tied to the economic conditions and/or the economy. For example, the Corona Virus led to people driving and traveling less. Less demand on transportation resulted in less demand for gasoline and other fuels which translated into lower costs per barrel of oil which is good for the consumer but not so good for those that invest in oil.

- **The company should not be heavily laden with debt**. I like companies that possess a total debt/equity ratio of 0.50 or less. A debt/equity ratio of 0.50 means that a company's total equity is twice that of its debt. In other words, the company's assets are double what it owes in total debt.

- **The company should possess financial strength and staying power.** I like to see a current ratio of 1.50 or greater as evidence of a company's financial strength and staying power.

- **The company's earnings per share (EPS) growth for the most recent five years should be positive.** This means that the company has managed to earn a profit each year during its most recent five-year period. Remember, earnings are the most important element when it comes to growth stocks. If earnings continue to climb year after year, so will the price of the stock.

- **The company should possess strong estimated future earnings per share growth prospects.** With this criteria, look for companies that are expected to grow their earnings per share 15% or more over the next five years.

- **The company's returns on equity (ROE) should be steady or growing.** Here, I like to see companies that have produced a five-year average return on equity of 15% or greater.

- **The companies should possess a low PEG ratio.** A company that possesses a PEG ratio of 1 is considered fairly valued. A company that possess a PEG ratio of more than 1 is considered overvalued and one with a PEG ratio of less than 1 is considered undervalued. So, look for companies that possess PEG ratios of less than 1. The lower the PEG ratio, the greater the margin of safety that a stock contains, thereby reducing investment risk. Unfortunately, with great growth stocks, it's hard to find them trading at a PEG ratio of less than 1 unless something is going on with the economy. So, I will consider investing in stocks that possess a PEG ratio under 2 since growth stocks usually trade up much higher valuations.

Don't rush with your money just so that it's invested in something. Take your time to find those growth stocks that are highly likely to become long-term winners. Using the criteria that has been outlined will assist you with identifying those growth stocks that possess the traits of long-term winners. The criteria that have been presented here can be screened using the FINVIZ screener, which has already been addressed earlier in this book. Of course, there are other screeners available that will work, but I specifically used the FINVIZ screener in my research and know that it's a very effective screener in my search for growth stocks. I have included a summary of the screening criteria in the table that follows. I also use Moringstar.com (free-version) to research the criteria explained that cannot be entered into the stock screener. For example, the stock screener wiil not tell you if a company has ten years of consistent operations, but that information along with much more information can be obtained at Morningstar.com and several other financial and investment websites.

THE WINNING GROWTH STOCK SCREEN

Country: USA

Market Capitalization: Minimum of $300 Million

Debt/Equity Ratio: Under 0.50

Current Ratio: 1.5 or greater

EPS Growth Rate (Past 5 Years): Positive

EPS Growth Est. (Next 5 Years): Over 15%

Return on Equity (Past 5 Years): Over +15%

PEG Ratio: Under 2

9

THE FINVIZ STOCK SCREENER
https://finviz.com/screener.ashx

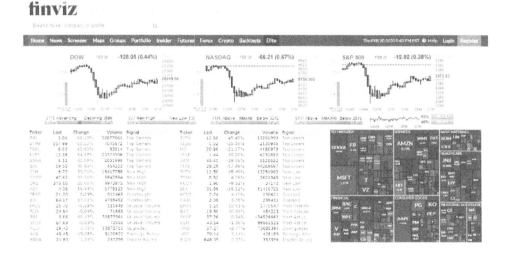

The FINVIZ stock screener is an online, browser-based stock screening tool that allows users to screen for stocks using a wide variety of descriptive, fundamental, and technical filters. The FINVIZ platform offers free and premium tools that traders and investors can use to generate stock investing ideas. I use only the free screening tool, and it easily meets my investment needs. The FINVIZ screener can be applied to many different trading or investing strategies, and is a very useful tool for both new and experienced traders and investors.

With a little familiarization, most users will find the FINVIZ platform to be user-friendly. The platform provides a sector performance tool, portfolio tracking, various charts and graphs, and numerous other features, which users may find valuable. I use the FINVIZ screener to assist me with fundamental analysis, but think the screener is an excellent choice for those desiring to perform technical analysis as well.

The FINVIZ screener contains approximately 7,700 stocks in its database. In addition to stocks, users can analyze specific sectors or indexes. Users should be aware that quotes received through the FINVIZ platform are delayed 20 minutes for the New York Stock Exchange (NYSE) and the American Stock Exchange (AMEX), and are delayed 15 minutes for the Nasdaq Stock Exchange unless users purchase the premium services offered by FINVIZ. First-time users can use the FINVIZ website without being required to log in or sign up to use the website, but will only have access to the website's basic features.

To access the more advanced features, the user must register on the website, which is a very simple and quick process. Users can also sign up for FINVIZ's Elite Plan which is the paid version. With it, users gain access to premium features not available to free or registered users. The FINVIZ screener is my favorite screener and the one that I mostly rely on during my research.

10

KEEP YOUR PORTFOLIO SMALL

Many investors are uncertain about how many stocks to hold in their portfolios and that's understandable, especially since the number of stocks contained in a portfolio usually play an important role in diversification and risk reduction. To make things even more complicated, there's so much information on this subject that seems contradictory at times. Don't fret. Studies have shown that investors who keep their portfolios small or concentrate their portfolios improve their chances of beating the market. Based on a great deal of personal research, I have drawn the conclusion that the small or individual investor's stock portfolio should contain a minimum of ten and a maximum of twenty stocks.

According to an article on *TheStreet.com*, dated Sept. 15, 2000, former hedge fund manager and best-selling author, Jim Cramer said he believes that the average person can only monitor about six stocks effectively in a portfolio. Cramer, undoubtedly, has a team of money managers helping him. That's probably why his charitable trust contains more than six stocks. Jim Slater, a famous investor from the

U.K., says the individual investor should hold a minimum of ten and a maximum of twelve stocks in his portfolio. Robert Hagstrom has performed extensive research into portfolio management. As he states in his book, *The Warren Buffett Portfolio*, "Your probability of beating the market goes up as the size of your portfolio goes down. With a 15-stock portfolio, you have a 1-in-4 chance of beating the market. With a 250-stock portfolio, your chances are 1 in 50."

Many years ago, I decided to do some research into the number of stocks contained in the portfolios of some of America's top money managers. I was only interested in those who had managed to obtain long-term returns above 15%. The results of my research are contained in the table that follows. Although this information was obtained several years ago and is no longer accurate, we can still learn something from it. Looking at the results of the table, we find that the long-term average annual rate of return for the portfolios listed is 23.3%, and the average number of stocks in these winning portfolios is twelve (when we exclude famed investor Robert Rodriquez, who did an amazing job with a portfolio containing a much larger number)

INVESTOR'S NAME	STOCKS HELD	LONG-TERM PERFORMANCE
Ian Cumming	5	33% annually from 1978-2004
Glenn Greenberg	12	23% annually from 1984-2004
Rober Karr	9	22% annually from 1996-2010
Seth Klarman	17	20% annually from inception in 1983
Edward Lampert	11	29% annually from 1988-2009
Mohnish Pabrai	17	29% annually from 1999-2006
David Swenson	10	17% annually for last ten years based on the date of the article.
Robert Rodriquez	25-45	17% annually from 1984-2007
Lou Simpson	13	20% annually from 1980-2004

It's difficult to argue against the results that these portfolios have achieved, although most are concentrated in the number of stocks that they contain. Dave Kansas, former editor-in-chief of *TheStreet.com,* once said, "For most people, the ability to follow more than a dozen stocks is likely limited. A portfolio of a dozen or so stocks should provide you with the protection of diversification and the focus to build wealth.

Jordan L. Kimmel – a leading investment expert and successful money manager – states in his book, *Magnet Investing,* "It only requires a handful of long-term profits in outstanding companies to create personal independent wealth." In other words, he is saying that owning stock shares in a few outstanding companies, over the long term, may be all it takes to become very wealthy.

By following the recommendations presented in this section, an investor should end up with a portfolio that is well-diversified. At the same time, the portfolio will not be so large that the investor has a hard time monitoring the stocks. Since your portfolio will be concentrated in number of stocks that it contain, pick only the best stocks available at your time of purchase, and be sure to purchase them with the all-important margin of safety.

11

HOW TO VALUE A GROWTH STOCK

My number one and favorite method for valuing growth stocks is the PEG ratio. I love the PEG ratio because it's simple to use, very precise, and allows me to quickly estimate the value of a growth stock. Jim Slater of the United Kingdom, an investment genius, is the creator of the PEG ratio. Peter Lynch and his management team greatly relied on the PEG ratio to help them pick undervalued stocks while he was at the helm of the Magellan Fund, where he racked up an impressive compounded rate of return of 29.2% annually for 13 years. A feat that is virtually unheard of in the investment world. What's even more amazing is that he accomplished this with a portfolio that contained thousands of stocks. Slater and Lynch are considered to be two of the world's greatest investors by many in the investment community.

There are a few drawbacks to using the PEG ratio just as there are with any of the stock valuation methods in use today. I will talk a little about two drawbacks that I think are of the utmost importance to any investor using the PEG ratio. The first is that the PEG ratio has proven to be unreliable when used to value large, mature companies and tends to punish those companies by assigning them values that are too low. Jim Slater states in his book, *Beyond the Zulu Principle,* that some of the best bargains are shares growing 25% annually and trading on a prospective P/E of 15. The term "prospective P/E" that's used by Slater is commonly referred to as the forward P/E here in the United States. So, the terms can be used interchangeably because they mean the same thing. In the same book, he also states that the PEG ratio should only be applied to growth stocks.

The other drawback is that the PEG ratio is limited by its focus on earnings growth. When Slater created the PEG ratio, it was never meant to be used alone, but to be used as an important tool during the fundamental analysis of a stock. It would be a mistake for any investor to buy a stock based solely on its earnings and earnings growth rate. Lynch's method of using the PEG ratio is slightly different from the manner in which Slater used it, but the end results are the same and those results are the identifying of undervalued growth stocks.

I apply the PEG ratio in the same manner that Lynch does because it actually places a monetary value on the individual stock being valued. It's the method that will be explained to you, but it's still basically the same PEG ratio that was created and used by Slater to find undervalued growth stocks. Slater referred to those undervalued stocks as "hidden gems." He defines the PEG ratio (Price/Earnings to Growth) as the relationship between the P/E ratio and its expected rate of earnings per share growth. The PEG ratio is calculated by dividing the prospective P/E of a stock by its estimated earnings growth rate, as demonstrated in the equation below:

$$\text{PEG Ratio} = \frac{\text{Price} / \text{Earnings}}{\text{Annual EPS Growth}}$$

Using this ratio, Slater believes that a fairly valued stock would trade at a PEG ratio of 1. Anything above 1 suggests that a stock is overvalued and anything below 1 indicates that a stock is undervalued. Basically, this means that any stock trading at a P/E equal to its estimated earnings growth rate should be considered fairly valued and any stock trading at a P/E lower than its estimated earnings growth rate should be considered undervalued. The manner in which Slater calculates a stock's PEG ratio results in a numerical value being assigned to that stock.

For example, let's say that you have a stock that has a prospective P/E of 15 that will grow its EPS by 30% over the next 5 years. He would take the P/E of 15 and divide it by 30, which is the EPS growth rate. The result of the calculation is 0.50 also known as the PEG by Slater. Since the resulting number is much lower than 1, then a stock with this particular PEG ratio would be considered extremely undervalued. As mentioned earlier, I use the PEG ratio in the same manner that Lynch does. So, let's take a look at it in action. Since the P/E ratio of any company that's fairly valued equals its growth rate, I replace the P/E ratio with the estimated earnings growth rate, and then I multiply the stock's estimated earnings per share by the estimated earnings growth rate. The following equation demonstrates exactly what I'm talking about.

(Next Year's Estimated EPS) X (Estimated Earnings Growth Rate) = Stock's Fair Value

Let's look at some examples of how the PEG ratio works so that you will better understand how to use it when valuing a growth stock. Looking at 2020 financial data for Axos Financial, Inc., an impressive internet banking company, we see that earnings are expected to grow at an annual rate of 10% for the next five years. Analysts also estimate that Axos Financial will earn $3.48 per share in 2021. Since the original PEG ratio states that a fairly valued stock should trade at a P/E ratio that's equal to its growth rate, this means that Axos Financial's trading at a P/E of 10 would be considered a fairly valued stock. Estimated earnings for 2021 are $3.48 per share. Multiplying those earnings by the P/E of 10 gives us a fair value of $34.80 per share using the PEG ratio. Axos Financial's current price on the stock market is $40.03, which means that the stock is overvalued based on the result of the PEG ratio.

Jim Slater said the brokers' consensus estimates are the most reliable future earnings and performed his PEG calculations on a rolling 12-month basis. There has been much debate concerning what time period to use when estimating the annual growth rate of stocks. You will usually find a recommendation of one-year forward earnings growth estimates to five-year earnings growth estimates. I prefer to use the five-year earnings growth estimates because I'm a long-term investor, and I believe that five-year growth estimates provide a cushion for stock market volatility.

Morningstar.com, zacks.com, money.msn.com, finance.yahoo.com, cnbc.com, and fool.com are some of my favorite sites to use for my research. You will probably only need to refer to one or two websites to obtain all the financial data that you will need to perform your stock analysis. The following are a few more examples of how to value a growth stock using the PEG ratio.

Next, we will look at Gentex Corporation, a high technology electronics company. Looking at Gentex Corporation's 2020 financial data, we find that Gentex Corporation earnings have grown at a rate of 11.1% annually for the last 5 years, and are expected to grow at an annual rate of 15.0% annually for the next five years. Analysts estimate that Gentex Corporation will earn $1.99 per share in 2021. The calculation would be as follows:

$1.99 (2021 EPS Estimate) X 15 (5 Year Earnings Growth Rate Estimate) = $29.85 (Fair Value)

At this point, I discount the fair value that I arrive at by 25%, meaning that I would look to buy Gentex Corporation for $22.39 per share or less. Of course, the lower the price, the more excited I get. This gives me the margin of safety that Benjamin Graham and Jim Slater have so often stressed in their writings, while at the same time, sets me up for those exceptional returns from buying the stock at a discount. Based on the PEG ratio, Gentex Corporation is overvalued at its current trading price of $34.00 per share.

$29.85 (Fair Value) X .75 (discount multiple) = $22.39 (Purchase Price)

Let's take a look at Apogee Enterprises Inc. Apogee Enterprises is a leader in glass fabrication and installation. Its products and services are used mainly in commercial buildings, institutional buildings, and multi-family residential buildings. Looking at Apogee Enterprises' 2020 financial data, we find that the company managed to grow its earnings at an annual rate of 6.10% for the previous five years, and analysts estimate that it will grow its earnings at 15.0% annually for the next five years. Analysts also estimate earnings of $2.34 per share for 2021.

$2.34 (2021 EPS Estimate) X 15 (5 Year Earnings Growth Rate Estimate) = $35.10 (Fair Value) $35.10 (Fair Value) X .75 (Discount Multiple) = $26.33 (Purchase Price)

Apogee Enterprises' current trading price is $35.49 per share. I would not buy it at its current price of $35.49 per share although that price since I'm looking for a margin of safety that comes with buying it at the discounted price of $26.33 per share.

Finally, we will look at LCI Industries Inc., a leading supplier of components to the recreational vehicles and residential housing industries, as well as adjacent industries, including bus, cargo, and equestrian trailer, marine, and heavy truck. LCI Industries' earnings per share have grown 17.9% annually for the last five years. Management has shown that it is efficient and effective with high returns on equity and high returns on capital over the same period. Looking at LCI Industries' 2020 financial data, we find that analysts expect earnings to grow at 20.0% annually over the next five years, and estimate that the company will earn $8.37 per share in 2021.

$8.37 (2021 EPS Estimate) x 20 (5 Year Earnings Growth Rate Estimate) = $167.40 (Fair Value)

$167.40 (Fair Value) X .75 (Discount Multiple) = $125.55 (Purchase Price)

LCI Industries' current trading price is $131.56 per share. Using the PEG ratio, we see that LCI Industries is slightly overvalued but it's a stock that I will keep a close watch on since it's very close to the discounted price of $125.55 per share.

If you are interested in learning more about the PEG ratio or using it in the same manner that Jim Slater uses it, I recommend that you read *The Zulu Principle* and *Beyond the Zulu Principle,* two excellent books written by the man himself. I actually created a practice portfolio and picked eight stocks for it using the PEG ratio in the manner that Slater does, and in about six months the portfolio had about a 40% gain, which is very impressive. All stocks in that practice portfolio were required to have PEG ratios of 0.60 or less.

The extraordinary success that Slater and Lynch have achieved through their use of the PEG ratio in their investment programs proves that it is a very effective tool when used to value growth stocks. I will leave you with a bit of wisdom from Benjamin Graham, the father of value investing. Graham said that if you are not certain a stock is worth its selling price, wait until it has fallen lower in price before purchasing it.

12

BEFORE YOU BUY A STOCK

I was once guilty of not doing what I'm about to recommend that you always do before you buy a stock. I was guilty of failing to check the most recent news about a company before I made my decision to purchase its stock. Now, I make it a priority to check the most recent news on a company before deciding whether or not I should purchase its stock. Although the performances of my portfolios have been extraordinary, perhaps they could have been better. Here's why. There have been more than a few stocks that I would not have bought, if only I had performed this news check beforehand.

For example, I would never have bought Life Partners Holdings Inc. many years ago, had I looked up its most recent news. There were numerous articles written by reputable financial columnists which warned that there were some serious problems within the company. The articles also mentioned that the company had questionable business practices. The columnists also advised that the situation was highly likely to get much worse, and they were right.

checked the articles and news only after I had purchased Life Partners Holdings, Inc. However, its stock price had already begun a deep descend into the abyss.

I am going to list several news items that should concern you as an investor, if the news has been reported to the public. If you learn that a company is involved or has become embroiled in any of the events detailed, your best course of action would be to put off buying the company's stock until you have thoroughly investigated the information. If the reported news is found to be true, you have the responsibility of determining from what you have learned, if the stock is worth purchasing or if you should move on to look for something else. Here's a list of news events that you should always investigate before buying the company's stock.

- Executive officer such as the Chief Executive Officer (CEO) or the Chief Financial Officer (CFO) quitting or being fired.
- Charges or accusations of corruption being rallied against the company's key personnel.
- Financial auditors quitting or being fired.
- Executive officers reported to be selling large quantities of their company stock.
- Announcements concerning an ongoing investigation of the company by federal or state officials.
- The majority of board members being replaced or fired (or quitting).
- Accusations of fraudulent accounting or other types of fraud being announced.

- Excessive compensation packages received by key personnel, despite the business steadily losing money.
- Large numbers of institutional investors reportedly selling their shares of the company's stock.
- Whistleblowers coming forward with information that could damage the company and its reputation.
- The company announcing that it will be issuing new shares to raise funds.
- Reports or announcements of buyouts or hostile takeovers of the company.

The list above is far from all-inclusive. It is your responsibility, as an investor, to stay alert. In the business world, circumstances can change quickly, and you must be able to change or adjust to those changes to be a very successful investor. By staying abreast of the most recent news, you will, at the very least, be up-to-date with a company's most recent activities. I believe that a news check will help you to avoid buying some bad investments (or investments that are about to turn bad). For me, one bad investment is one too many.

13

USING LIMIT ORDERS

There are several types of buy and sell orders available to investors and some can be more than a little confusing to understand. Luckily for us, there are only two types that the growth stock investor needs to be concerned with: *market orders* and *limit orders*.

A market order is defined as an order to buy or sell a stock at the best available price. With market orders, the order is generally executed quickly but the drawback is that the price at which a market order will be executed is not guaranteed. In other words, when using market orders, it is possible to pay more for a stock that you are buying or receive less for a stock that you are selling than you planned. If there's a sudden drop or rise in the stock market, market orders can be impacted dramatically.

For example, let's suppose that you place a market order to buy a certain stock when the stock market opens because it closed on the previous day at a trading price of $30 per share. Before the market opens, the company reports better than expected earnings and revenue resulting in the stock immediately rising to $40 per share at the markets open. Guess what? There's a very high probability that you will end up paying $40 per share for stock that you were planning to purchase for $30 per share resulting in you paying 33% more for the shares than you had originally planned. Selling can work the same way. The market falls dramatically upon opening, and your shares are sold for a lot less than you had desired. That's the dangers that come with using market orders.

A limit order is defined as an order to buy or sell a stock at a specific price or better. The drawback to using limit orders is that they can only be filled if the stock market's price reaches the limit price and the numbers of shares desired are available for purchase. The advantage of using limit orders is that they prevent an investor from paying more than he or she desires for a stock being purchased and guarantee that he or she will receive the price desired or a better one for the stock that is being sold if the trade executes.

In the past, I used both types of orders but now I place only limit orders because an investor is always better off using limit orders when buying or selling shares of any stocks. Placing or using market orders is usually a losing proposition, and will more than likely work to the investor's disadvantage. So, I believe that the intelligent investor should use limit orders when buying and selling stocks. That way, the deal works in his or her favor instead of someone else's.

14

SELLING A GROWTH STOCK

G rowth stock investing is long-term investing and the same sell strategies that apply to most other long-term investment styles also apply to growth investing. Determining when to sell a stock is much harder than determining when to buy one because sometimes a stock that appears to be overvalued can continue to rise in price for many years, and increase in value several thousand percentages from the original purchase price.

Even the world's best investors wrestle with determining when to sell a stock and most will admit it's much easier to decide when to buy, than when to sell. Author Robert Hagstrom has written several excellent books about Warren Buffett and his investment strategies. In *The Warren Buffett Portfolio*, he says that an investor should leave his or her portfolio intact for at least five years, as long as the fundamentals for which a particular stock was purchased do not deteriorate. He also says investors should pay no attention to a stock's price volatility because it is a normal part of the investment cycle.

In their book *Million Dollar Portfolio*, the Motley Fool team says investors' minimum holding period for each stock that is purchased should be three to five years. As a long-term investor, there will be times when it makes sense to sell or reduce your position in a stock earlier than you had planned. Next, we will talk about different circumstances in which you should consider selling a stock or at the very least, reducing your position in it.

The Time Frame - If you will need the money within five years, it should not be invested in stocks. It would be best to invest your money in safe and stable short-term instruments. Savings accounts, money market accounts, money market funds, and short-term certificates of deposits would probably be better options.

An Overvalued Stock - When a stock is significantly overvalued, sell it. Take the proceeds from the sale and invest them into other undervalued stocks that you have researched. For growth stocks, The PEG ratio is the best indicator of value. I'm slow to sell an overvalued stock if it's not extremely overvalued because excellent investment choices are hard to find.

Too Much Debt - Too much debt is dangerous for any business because there's always the chance that a business may be unable to pay its debt. Too much debt also puts a business at greater risk of failure if a downturn in the industry or economy were to occur. Upon entering the 2007 recession, thousands of businesses here in the United States literally disappeared overnight and that was before things really got bad. I'm willing to bet that those businesses that were carrying too much debt were the first to go.

When looking at the debt of a company, I like to look at how the company has handled its debt over the long-term. For example, I will look at its annual debt-to-equity ratios for the last ten years. If the company has managed to keep its debt-to-equity ratio within a specific range and all of a sudden its ratio moves way above that range, I will take a serious look at the company to try to determine what's going on. Normally, I like companies with debt-to-equity ratios of 1.00 or less; but that rule cannot be applied to all companies. There are many solid and financially sound companies that carry debt-to-equity ratios that are much higher. So, it's also a good idea to look at a company's historical debt-to-equity ratios over the last 7 to 10 years to see if it's normal or if it's out of the ordinary.

Too Much Risk - Sometimes new management will come to a business and begin to implement new policies; along with that implementation, they will knowingly or unknowingly expose a business to greater risk. If you purchased the stock of a company that avoided very risky practices, but the company has recently displayed risky behaviors that make you uncomfortable, sell the stock and find yourself a better investment.

Loss of Competitive Advantage – We should only be purchasing the stocks of companies that have a durable competitive advantage. When a company changes its business model, resulting in it losing its competitive advantage, sell the stock. A durable competitive is a very important element that's found in many of the most successful companies around the world.

The Portfolio Lacks Balance or Diversification - It's very easy for your best performing stock to become the largest holding in your portfolio, and there's absolutely nothing wrong with that. The problem arises when the stock makes up more than 20-25% of your portfolio's total value. I would be very uncomfortable having more than 25% of my portfolio's value tied to just one stock. Legendary investor, Jim Slater suggests that individual investors limit the number of funds invested in a single stock within their portfolios to a maximum of 15%. When your portfolio becomes heavily weighted in one stock, consider reducing your position of that stock to bring more balance and better diversification into your portfolio.

When Your Analysis is Found to Be Flawed- There will be times when an investor will be very detailed and careful in his or her analysis of a particular company or its stock, only to find out later that his or her analysis is incorrect or flawed. Whether a stock should be sold at that time depends on the seriousness of the error and its impact on the long-term performance of the business. So, when you find that you have incorrectly analyzed a particular company, it is essential for you to look at all available information to determine whether or not to sell the stock or to continue holding it. One thing is certain, as an investor, you will not always be right when analyzing a company or its stock.

15

PHILIP FISHER'S THREE YEAR RULE

When I consider the great investors, I cannot think of any that implements a short-term investment strategy. Since they don't, why should we? Many years ago, it was common for the average investor to actually hold a stock for several years or invest for the long-term but it's unfortunate that those days are long gone. Long-term investing for many of today's investors may be considered a few hours, days, or weeks.

In his book *Common Stocks And Uncommon Profits,* investing pioneer Philip A. Fisher said that if an investor had done his or her job correctly when purchasing a common stock, the time to sell was almost never. Fisher found that when investors held the right stocks for long periods of time, even in bad markets, they were usually rewarded with returns of several hundred or several thousand percent. Fisher was one who practiced what he preached by refusing to sell even those stocks from his portfolios that would have appeared to be overvalued by today's standards or measures. He held shares of Motorola for more than forty years. According to Fisher, every $1000 that he and his clients invested in Motorola in 1957 was worth $1,993,846 a few decades later. Fisher found that those investors that sold very good stocks from their portfolios that they perceived to be overvalued in an effort to buy them back once they had fallen in price usually didn't get the opportunity to do so. He found that those stocks usually went on to reach new highs.

This section stresses the importance of having a long-term frame of mind when it comes to investing in individual stocks. More specifically, it's about having a Philip A. Fisher frame of mind when it comes to holding growth stocks. In *Common Stocks and Uncommon Profits,* Fisher says that he established himself a three-year rule. Under his rule, Fisher asked his clients whose portfolios he managed, to give him three years before judging his performance. He told them that if he had failed to produce satisfactory results for them at the end of three years, they should fire him. Now, I must admit that I have the slightest idea of what kind of performance Fisher or the clients expected. No doubt, it was some measure or goal that they had agreed to in advance. Fisher also applied his three-year rule to his management of individual stocks. When applied to stocks, he was determined to hold an individual stock for a minimum of three years regardless of how good or bad the stock had performed as long as nothing had happened to change his original view about the company. Even for those stocks that had risen significantly in price, he still adhered to his three-year rule.

Through research, I found some other great investors that also adhere to a three-year rule in a similar manner like Fisher. For example, the Motley Fool Team says that investors' minimum holding period for each stock purchased should be three to five years. As further evidence of support for the three-year rule, look at the following quote by great investor David Dreman."If you have good stocks and really know them, you'll make money if you're patient over three years or more."

Therefore it makes sense to consider Fisher's three-year rule. If Fisher's three-year rule teaches us nothing else, it certainly teaches us the importance of patience when it comes to investing. There's no doubt that most investors could use a little more patience which is a necessity for successful investing and it is patience that sets the world's greatest investors apart from everyone else. Lastly, I don't think we could go wrong with the implementation of Fisher's three-year rule into our investment plan or investment program.

16

JAMES D. SLATER:
GROWTH STOCK INVESTOR

J ames D. Slater was a very successful United Kingdom (U.K businessman, investor, author, and financial columnist, was bor in the U.K. on March 13, 1929. He is one of the U.K.'s mos successful investors and has often been referred to as the "Warre Buffett of the U.K." Slater is credited for creating the PEG ratio an helping to popularize its use in the United Kingdom and the Unite States.

At the age of 24, Slater joined Dohm Group and quickly advance through the ranks to become a general manager. After leaving Dohr Group, he went to work for Park Royal Vehicles where he wa promoted to Commercial Director of its subsidiary named AEC. Whil at AEC, Slater became very ill and it was doing his recovery from hi illness that he took an interest in investing. It was also during this tim that he developed his stock investing system that he explains in hi book *The Zulu Principle*.

In 1964, Slater and Peter Walker acquired Lotery & Company Limited and renamed it Slater Walker Securities. Within a very short time, Slater and Walker managed to build Slater Walker Securities into a financial powerhouse that had amazing success in the 1960s and early 1970s. During the United Kingdom's banking crisis of 1975, Slater Walker Securities faced financial difficulties that resulted in it receiving financial assistance from the Bank of England. Slater resigned as Chairman in October of 1975 and the company was eventually taken over by the Bank of England. The collapse of Slater Walker Securities bankrupted Slater, yet he managed to regain his solvency through private investing of the remaining funds left after the bankruptcy. Following the bankruptcy, Slater also started a new career as a financial writer.

After the troubles with Slater Walker Securities, Slater went on to form several successful ventures that helped him to recover financially while earning substantial profits along the way. As a financial writer, he became very popular in the United Kingdom through his column in the *Sunday Telegraph* where he wrote under the pen-name "Capitalist." Because of his articles, his investment methodology was one of the first to be made widely available to the general public in the United Kingdom.

Slater believed that the small or individual investor stood a better chance of obtaining extraordinary returns by researching and investing in the stocks of smaller companies that the leading brokers wouldn't bother researching. Slater referred to those small-cap stocks (stocks of small companies) as *Hidden Gems*. He along with Hemmington Scott developed Company REFS to help private investors identify such stocks. Long before his death, Slater was once again a popular figure and a household name in the United Kingdom. James D. Slater died November 18, 2015, at the age of 86, and had remained active in business and investing until his death.

James D. Slater wrote several excellent books that I have enjoyed reading. I have read *The Zulu Principle*, *Beyond the Zulu Principle,* and *How to Become a Millionaire, reading each of them more than once.*

17

SCREENING FOR ZULU TYPE STOCKS

This screen looks to identify stocks based on the criteria outlined in James Slater's book *The Zulu Principle.* Slater believed that the private investor should focus on companies that were capable of growing their earning from 15% to 25% yearly and that the greatest profits could be realized by investing in small and medium-sized companies that were ignored by leading brokers. Slater also recommends that the private investor verify that the company has healthy profit margins and shareholder-friendly management. He believed that companies in which management-owned at least 20% of the company are good indicators of companies with management that's shareholder-friendly.

THE ZULU STOCK SCREEN

Country: USA

Market Capitalization: +Micro (Over $50 Million)

PEG Ratio: Less than 1

EPS Growth Rate (Next 5 Years): Over 20%

Return on Equity (Past 5 Years): Over +15%

Debt/Equity Ratio: Less than 0.50

Net Profit Margin: Over 5%

Insider Ownership: Over 20%

18

PETER LYNCH: GROWTH STOCK INVESTOR

Peter Lynch is an American Investor and philanthropist, considered by many in the investment community to be one of the greatest and most successful investors of all time. Lynch was born on January 19, 1944, in Newton, Massachusetts. He attended Boston College and graduated with a degree in finance in 1965. After graduation, he served in the United States Army from 1967 to 1969. He furthered his education by attending the Wharton School at the University of Pennsylvania where he graduated with a Masters of Business Administration degree in 1968.

Lynch went to work for Fidelity Investments in 1966 and worked for the company until his retirement in 1990. He started as an analyst in the paper, chemicals, and publishing industries at Fidelity and served as Director of Research from 1974 to 1977. In 1977, he was given the job of managing the Fidelity Magellan Fund and did so for 13 years. While at the helm of the Magellan Fund, he achieved an amazing annual average return of 29.2% for his investors. Every $10,000 invested with Lynch at the beginning of his tenure was worth

$280,000 when he retired from managing the fund. To date, no other mutual fund manager has been able to achieve the feat of posting long-term returns that match those of Lynch and the Magellan Fund. It is considered the most successful mutual fund in mutual fund history. What's even more impressive is the fact that Lynch achieved his amazing returns with a portfolio that contained more than 1000 stocks and at times the portfolio contained more than 1400 stocks.

Lynch was perhaps, the first American investor to use the PEG ratio to determine if a company was undervalued or overvalued, and can be credited with the popularity of the PEG ratio use in the United States today. Lynch also coined the term "ten-baggers", which was the term used to describe an investment that had appreciated to the point of being worth ten times its cost. According to an article in Forbes Magazine, Lynch bought more than 100 ten-baggers while running the Magellan Fund.

Lynch was truly one that was willing to think outside the box. In addition to growth stocks (referred to as fast growers by Lynch), he invested in stalwarts, turnarounds, slow growers, cyclicals, and asset plays. Because Lynch was very successful at picking many top-performing growth stocks, and he looked to buy shares in growth stocks when he determined them to be undervalued. Lynch also stressed the importance of buying what you know, meaning that you should only invest in businesses that you understand. Also, he wanted the business to have good and honest management in place some type of competitive advantage, and little to no debt.

Lynch has authored several books but his most popular books are *One Up On Wall Street* and *Beating the Street*. Both are books I have read and think they are excellent for anyone wanting to learn how to become a better investor. Currently, Lynch focuses much of his time on philanthropy and co-founded the Lynch Foundation with his wife Carolyn who died in October of 2015. He also serves as a Vice-Chairman at Fidelity Management and Research Company.

19

SCREENING FOR LYNCH TYPE STOCKS

I n Peter Lynch's book *One Up On Wall Street,* he classifies stocks into six different categories for the investor to consider. Those categories are slow growers, fast growers, stalwarts, cyclicals, asset plays, and turnarounds. This screen looks for fast growers since they are the companies that offer the greatest return potential to the individual or small investor and tend to be much easier to understand than cyclicals, asset plays, and turnarounds. Fast growers are the land of the "*ten baggers*", and during his career, Lynch bought more than 100 *ten baggers*. Good examples of companies that use to be classified as fast growers are Amazon, eBay, Starbucks, Microsoft, Wal-Mart, and Coca-Cola. By choosing companies with market capitalizations (market caps) under 10 billion, we have a larger selection of stocks to choose from since this selection includes small and micro-cap companies too.

THE LYNCH SCREEN

Country: USA

Market Capitalization: Under 10 BillionPEG

Ratio: Less than 1

EPS Growth Rate (Past 5 Years): Over 20%

Return on Equity (Past 5 Years): Over +15%

Debt/Equity Ratio: Less than 0.40

Current Ratio: 1.5 or greater

20

DISCLAIMER

The author or publisher is not engaged in rendering legal, accounting, investment, or other professional services. Investing in stocks and the stock market involves varying degrees of risk, and there's no assurance that a specific stock, investment principle, or investment strategy will be profitable for an individual, group, or organization. Although the 10 Stocks listed in the "10 Great Stocks for the Long Run" section may meet certain criteria set forth in this book titled, it's not a recommendation from the author or publisher to purchase or sell any of the stocks discussed herein. A stock's past performance does not guarantee similar future results.

All information contained in this book was gathered from sources believed to be reliable, but neither the author nor the publisher can accept responsibility for its accuracy. The author or publisher specifically disclaim any responsibility for liability, loss, or risk, professional or otherwise, which is incurred as a consequence, directly or indirectly, of the use and application of any of the contents of this book.

Note: Financial information provided for each company is based on the company's most recently reported full five-year period.

21

10 GREAT GROWTH STOCKS FOR THE LONG RUN

S mall-cap and mid-cap growth stocks are stocks of fast-growing businesses with market capitalizations of starting around $300 million and ending in the $10 billion range. Small and mid-cap growth stocks can be expected to generate above-average revenue and earnings. The increases in revenue and earnings are very important because they translate into greater returns for the shareholders. These fast-growing businesses have significant room for growth in size, revenue, and most importantly, earnings.

James D. Slater a very successful United Kingdom (U.K.) investor, believed that the small or individual investor stood a better chance of obtaining extraordinary returns by researching and investing in the stocks of smaller companies that the leading brokers wouldn't bother researching. Slater referred to the small-cap stocks (stocks of small companies) as *Hidden Gems*.

In 1999, Warren Buffett told the shareholders at the annual meeting for Berkshire Hathaway that he could generate 50% annual returns for the shareholders, if only he had less money to invest

Having smaller amounts of money to invest gives us an advantage, even over Buffett and Munger, since we are able to invest in the smaller, faster-growing companies that have the potential to provide the greatest returns to investors.

Buffett and Munger have such large amounts of money to manage, that investing in the small, fast-growing companies would hardly make any kind of impact on Berkshire Hathaway's portfolio. In other words, if Buffett or Munger invested in smaller businesses, this investment would have very little effect on the total return of the portfolio. It probably would not be worth their time. There's a good possibility that these smaller companies are worth it for us! One important thing that I need to mention is that there is an opportunity to make lots of money by investing in companies with larger market capitalizations as well since many of those can be classified as growth stocks. So, you will find that the ten stocks presented here possess a variety of market caps, although with all things being equal, the greatest potential returns lie in the small and mid-cap stock arena.

Apogee Enterprises Inc. (APOG) #1

Apogee Enterprises, Inc. is a leader in glass fabrication and installation. Its products and services are used mainly in commercial buildings, institutional buildings, and multi-family residential buildings. Apogee Enterprises, Inc. is organized into four segments, with three segments serving the commercial construction market. In 2020, Apogee Enterprise achieved revenue of $1.38 billion. Apogee Enterprises, Inc. was founded in 1949 and is headquartered in Minneapolis, Minnesota.

Apogee Enterprises has grown its earnings-per-share (EPS) at an annual rate of 6.10% during its most recent five-year period. The company has achieved an average annual return on equity (ROE) of 14.8% and an average annual return on capital (ROC) of 12.40% during the last five years. The company has a current ratio of 1.60 and a debt-to-equity ratio of 0.31 as of February 12, 2021. The company is expected to grow its earnings-per-share at an annual rate of 15.00% over the long-term. Apogee Enterprises currently pays an annual dividend of 2.91%.

Carlisle Companies, Inc. (CSL) #2

Carlisle Companies, Inc. operates as a diversified manufacturing company with a global portfolio of niche brands and businesses. The company operates in five segments: Carlisle Brake & Friction, Carlisle Construction Materials, Carlisle Fluid Technologies, Carlisle FoodService Products, and Carlisle Interconnect Technologies. In 2020, Carlisle Companies, Inc. generated revenue of $4.25 billion. Carlisle Companies, Inc. was founded in 1917 and is headquartered in Scottsdale, Arizona.

Carlisle Companies has grown its earnings-per-share (EPS) at an annual rate of 3.90% during its most recent five-year period. The company has obtained an average annual return on equity (ROE) of 15.80% and an average annual return on capital (ROC) of 11.16% during the last five years. The company has a current ratio of 3.40 and a debt-to-equity ratio of 0.82 as of March 16, 2021. The company is expected to grow its earnings-per-share at an annual rate of 15.00% over the long-term. The company currently pays an annual dividend of 1.32%.

Copart, Inc. (CPRT) #3

Copart, Inc. is a global leader in online vehicle auctions and a premier destination for resale and remarketing of vehicles. Copart, Inc. operates through two segments: The United States and International. It currently operates more than 200 locations in 11 countries and has over 175,000 vehicles up for auction every day. Copart, Inc. was founded in 1982 and is headquartered in Dallas, Texas.

Copart, Inc., has grown its earnings-per-share (EPS) at an annual rate of 28.50%% during its most recent five-year period. The company has obtained an average annual return on equity (ROE) of 34.49% and an average annual return on capital (ROC) of 25.10% during the last five years. The company has a current ratio of 3.30 and a debt-to-equity ratio of 0.14 as of March 16, 2021. The company is expected to grow its earnings-per-share at an annual rate of 28.50% over the long-term. Copart, Inc. currently does not pay a dividend.

Dollar General Corp. (DG) #4

Dollar General has become America's neighborhood general store with more than 17,000 stores in 46 states. Dollar General Stores are strategically located in small towns or rural neighborhoods, which gives them an advantage over larger discount retailers such as Wal-Mart. Dollar General separates its merchandise into four categories: Highly Consumable, Home Products, Basic Clothing, and Seasonal. Dollar General Stores sell a broad selection of products such as housewares, food, cleaning supplies, pet products, personal care items, and automotive supplies. Dollar General Corp. was founded in 1939 and is headquartered in Goodlettsville, Tennessee.

Dollar General has grown its earnings-per-share (EPS) at an annual rate of 13.70%% during its most recent five-year period. The company has obtained an average annual return on equity (ROE) of 24.47% and an average annual return on capital (ROC) of 15.86% during the last five years. The company has a current ratio of 1.30 and no debt as of March 16, 2021. The company is expected to grow its earnings-per-share at an annual rate of 17.31% over the long-term. Dollar General Corp. currently pays an annual dividend of 0.74%.

Gentex Corp. (GNTX) #5

Gentex Corp. is a high technology electronics company that specializes in a broad spectrum of technologies and processes to deliver high-quality products to the automotive, aerospace, and fire protection industries. Gentex Corp. sells its products worldwide. The company was founded in 1974 and is headquartered in Zeeland, Michigan.

Gentex Corp. has grown its earnings-per-share (EPS) at an annual rate of 11.10% during its most recent five-year period. The company has achieved an average annual return on equity (ROE) of 20.80% and an average annual return on capital (ROC) of 19.60% during the last five years. The company has a current ratio of 4.10 and no debt as of February 12, 2021. The company is expected to grow its earnings-per-share at an annual rate of 15.00% over the long-term. Gentex Corp. currently pays an annual dividend of 1.67%.

LCI Industries, Inc. (LCII) #6

LCI Industries, Inc. is a leading supplier of components to the recreational vehicle and residential housing industries; as well as adjacent industries, including bus, cargo and equestrian trailer, marine, and heavy truck. LCI Industries, Inc. sells its products in the U.S. and internationally. The company operates through two segments: Original Equipment Manufacturers (OEM) and Aftermarket. LCI Industries was founded in 1962 and is based in Elkhart, Indiana.

LCI Industries has grown its earnings-per-share (EPS) at an annual rate of 17.90% during its most recent five-year period. The company has achieved an average annual return on equity (ROE) of 21.50% and an average annual return on capital (ROC) of 18.10% during the last five years. The company has a current ratio of 2.00 and a debt-to-equity ratio of 0.73 as of February 12, 2021. The company is expected to grow its earnings per share at an annual rate of 20.00% over the long-term and currently pays an annual dividend of 2.71%.

National Beverage Corp. (FIZZ) #7

National Beverage Corp. is a leader in the development, manufacturing, marketing, and sale of a diverse portfolio of flavored beverage products including sparkling waters, juices, energy drinks, and carbonated soft drinks. National Beverage Corp. is the 4th largest branded carbonated soft-drink company in the U.S. It has twelve manufacturing facilities strategically located in major metropolitan markets throughout the U.S. National Beverage Corp. was founded in 1985 and is headquartered in Fort Lauderdale, Florida.

National Beverage Corp. has grown its earnings-per-share (EPS) at an annual rate of 21.40% during its most recent five-year period. The company has achieved an average annual return on equity (ROE) of 41.91% and an average annual return on capital (ROC) of 41.21% during the last five years. The company has a current ratio of 2.40 and no debt as of March 16, 2021. The company is expected to grow its earnings-per-share at an annual rate of 25.56% over the long-term. National Beverage Corp. currently pays no dividend.

ResMed, Inc. (RMD) #8

ResMed, Inc. is a world-leading medical equipment company that is engaged in developing, manufacturing, and distributing medical devices and cloud-based software solutions for diagnosing, treating, and managing sleep apnea, chronic obstructive pulmonary disease, and other respiratory diseases. ResMed, Inc. distributes its products in approximately 120 countries through wholly-owned and independent businesses. The company was founded in 1989 and is headquartered in San Diego, California.

ResMed Inc. has grown its earnings-per-share (EPS) at an annual rate of 11.50% during its most recent five-year period. The company has achieved an average annual return on equity (ROE) of 20.54% and an average annual return on capital (ROC) of 14.36% during the last five years. The company has a current ratio of 2.50 and a debt-equity ratio of 0.29 as of March 16, 2021. The company is expected to grow its earnings-per-share at an annual rate of 22.10% over the long-term and currently pays an annual dividend of 0.81%.

Thor Industries, Inc. (THO) #9

Thor Industries, Inc., through its subsidiaries, designs, manufacturers, and sells RVs (recreational vehicles) and related parts. Thor Industries is the world's largest supplier of RVs with over 50% market share for towables and more than 40% market share for motorhomes. The company operates through two segments: Towable Recreational Vehicles and Motorized Recreational Vehicles. Its RVs are sold through independent dealers in the U.S. and Canada. Thor Industries, Inc. had revenue of $8.17 billion in 2020. The company was founded in 1980 and is based in Elkhart, Indiana.

Thor Industries has grown its earnings-per-share (EPS) at an annual rate of 1.20% during its most recent five-year period. The company has achieved an average annual return on equity (ROE) of 18.11% and an average annual return on capital (ROC) of 15.42% during the last five years. The company has a current ratio of 1.50 and a debt-equity ratio of 0.73 as of March 16, 2021. The company is expected to grow its earnings-per-share at an annual rate of 24.40% over the long-term and currently pay an annual dividend of 1.11%.

Ulta Beauty, Inc. (ULTA) #10

Ulta Beauty, Inc. is the largest beauty retailer in the U.S. The company offers more than 20,000 products, including cosmetics, fragrance, hair and skin-care products, styling tools, and accessories. The company also produces Ulta Beauty's own private label and has a full-service salon in every store. Ulta Beauty, Inc. operates approximately 1264 retail stores in 50 states and the District of Columbia. Ulta Beauty, Inc. was founded in 1990 and is based in Bolingbrook, Illinois.

Ulta Beauty, Inc. has grown its earnings-per-share (EPS) at an annual rate of 25.00% during its most recent five-year period. The company has achieved an average annual return on equity (ROE) of 30.23% and an average annual return on capital (ROC) of 24.91% during the last five years. The company has a current ratio of 1.80 and no debt as of March 16, 2021. Ulta Beauty, Inc. is expected to grow its earnings-per-share at an annual rate of 41.80% over the long-term and currently pays no dividend.

Hello Fellow Investor,

Thank you so much for reading *A Beginner's Guide to Growth Stock Investing*. I hope you enjoyed reading the book as much as I enjoyed researching and writing it. It has been a delight to share with you knowledge I have gained through almost two decades of research, study and portfolio management. If you like this book and have a minute to spare, please consider writing a review on the page or website from which you bought the book. Even if you didn't like it, I would appreciate your feedback.

I have provided the link for Amazon below. Thank you so much for reading my book.

In gratitude,

James Pattersenn Jr.

Amazon Link:

https://www.amazon.com/review/create-review/listing

YOUR FREE GIFT

Thanks for buying my book. As a way of showing my appreciation, I'd like to give you something. It won't cost you a penny! It's my PDF report titled *5 Stocks That Warren Buffett Would Love.*

I'd like you to have a copy with my compliments.

Contained within this report are:

- 5 wonderful companies that Warren Buffett might buy today if given the opportunity.
- The specific criteria for picking Buffett-type stocks via value investing.
- Great companies that are practically guaranteed to grow and deliver big returns well beyond the pandemic!

Claim your copy of *5 Stocks That Warren Buffett Would Love* by clicking the link below and joining my mailing list. As added bonus to being on my mailing list, I will alert you when I release a new book. Since my new releases are usually free or selling at a steep discount for the first 24 to 48 hours, you'll be the first to know.

https:/ mailchi.mp/b65776af6219/5-stocks-warren-buffett-would-love

OTHER BOOKS BY JAMES PATTERSENN JR

You Can Invest Like A Stock Market Pro:
How to Use Simple and Powerful Strategies of the World's Greatest Investors to Build Wealth

Now That You Can Invest Like a Pro:
More Principles and Strategies for Building Wealth Like the World's Greatest Investors

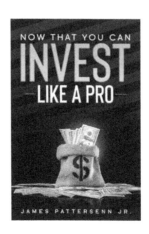

Common Sense Investing With Stock Screeners:

Make Stock Investing a Safe Bet with the Right Tools

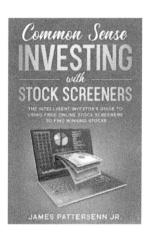

100 Stocks That a Young Warren Buffett Might Buy:

Proven Methods for Buying Stocks and Building Wealth

Like Warren Buffett and Charlie Munger

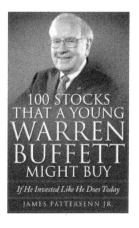

Common Sense Investing With Index Funds

How to Build Wealth, Achieve Financial Freedom, and Outperform Most Amateur and Professional Investors Without Really Trying!

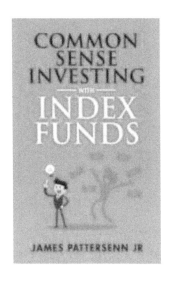

THE AUTHOR

James Pattersenn Jr. is a self-taught private investor and investment researcher that literally spent thousands of hours performing research to determine what does and doesn't work when investing in stocks and the stock market. He has put into practice what he has learned about investing using his own money and says that the investment strategies work, and they work very well.

Pattersenn is a graduate of York Technical College with Honors. He has also extensively studied courses in Business Administration while attending the institution and has earned numerous college credits in the process. He also earned an Undergraduate Certificate in Criminal Justice with Honors from Ashworth College.

Pattersenn served four years in the United States Marine Corps where he was meritoriously promoted twice and received an Honorable Discharge and Good Conduct Award. He was recalled to active duty to serve during Operation Desert Storm and received the National Defense Service Medal as a result.

He enjoys exercising and was a competitive powerlifter many years ago and took first place in the North Carolina State Powerlifting

Championship in the 181 pounds class. He now speed walks about every day and practices the martial art known as Hapkido. He was born and resides in the beautiful state of South Carolina with his family.

ACKNOWLEDGEMENTS

My sincere thanks to:

Carrie Pattersenn, my sweet and unselfish mother. She taught me the importance of putting the needs of others before my own if I truly wanted to be blessed and to be a blessing.

The great investors who have made this book and all my other books possible because they cared enough to willingly share their wisdom and knowledge about investing with the rest of us.

Timason, a professional graphic artist and engineer, whom I discovered at Fiverr. I'm always very happy with the excellent job that he does formatting my books. He does high-quality work at such affordable prices. I will continue to hire him for all of my future projects. He can be found on Fiverr where he has been a member for more than five years with a perfect 5-Star rating! He can be contacted at https://www.fiverr.com/inbox/tlmason

Proof Royalty, a professional proofreading service that does an excellent job of improving my writing to make me look smarter than I really am! Proof Royalty can be contacted at https://www.fiverr.com/inbox/proof_royalty

Snirz94, a book publishing expert gifted with more book publishing and book marketing skills then I have time to write about. With his unique combination of skills, he focuses on publishing, marketing, and sales. He can be contacted at https://www.fiverr.com/snirz94

Most of all, I thank God, the Father, and my Lord Jesus Christ, who is gracious and merciful to all.

Made in United States
North Haven, CT
05 March 2022

16835415R00055